Presented to:

_____

Presented by:

_____

Date:

_____

Love is like swallowing hot chocolate
before it has cooled off.
It takes you by surprise at first,
but keeps you warm for a long time.

AUTHOR UNKNOWN

Fun & Creative Dates

for Dating Couples

52 Ways to Have Fun Together!

HOWARD BOOKS
A DIVISION OF SIMON & SCHUSTER
New York   London   Toronto   Sydney

Published by Howard Books, a division of Simon & Schuster, Inc.
1230 Avenue of the Americas, New York, NY 10020

Fun & Creative Dates for Dating Couples—52 Ways to Have Fun Together! © 2008 by Dave Bordon and Associates, LLC

Library of Congress Cataloging-in-Publication Data

Fun & creative dates for dating couples : 52 ways to have fun together!
    p. cm.
  1. Dating (Social customs) 2. Couples—Recreation. I. Title: Fun and creative dates for dating couples.
    HQ801.F86 2008
    306.73—dc22

                                                            2008013660

ISBN-13: 978-1-4165-6496-6
ISBN-10:   1-4165-6496-9

10 9 8 7 6 5 4 3

Manufactured in the United States of America

For information regarding special discounts for bulk purchases, please contact: Simon & Schuster Special Sales at 1-800-456-6798 or business@simonandschuster.com.

Project developed by Bordon Books, Tulsa, Oklahoma
Project writing and compilation: Christy Phillippe, Shawna McMurry, and Rayné Bordon in association with Bordon Books; Rebecca Currington in association with Snapdragon Group℠ Editorial Services
Edited by Chrys Howard
Cover and interior design by Lori Jackson, LJ Designs
Illustrations by Vanda Grigorovic

Introduction

Dating. Where do you go and what do you do together while you're learning about each other, waiting to see if this is the *one*?

If you and your date ask these questions, this little book could be the answer to your prayers. Inside, there are fifty-two (one for each week) suggestions for great dates. Many are inexpensive or cost nothing at all. Others will require you to plan carefully and put some money away. There are fun dates, reflective dates, extreme dates, dates that focus on conversation—all kinds of dates. Each one contains that magical element we call adventure or fun.

You'll discover great ideas to maximize your time together, and you'll see how much fun dating can be!

Contents

The giving of love is
an education in itself.

ELEANOR ROOSEVELT

1. Alphabet Date

Simple and entertaining, this makes a perfect first date. Choose a letter—any letter. Putting all the letters in a hat and drawing one out is a great way to decide. Then agree that everything you do on your date will begin with that letter. For example, if your letter is "m," you will want to go to a movie or museum. If your letter is "w," you might go window-shopping or waterskiing. Carry this theme throughout the night with every place you go and everything you do. It will soon become a challenge, but one that you will have a great time figuring out together.

Make the suggestion for this date before the big night. That way no one will have made plans that have to be scrapped.

Budget

$ Depends on what letter you choose and what you want to make of it.

Steps to Success

- Take along a pocket dictionary—you'll need it.

- Dress for any eventuality you may encounter.

- Set your ground rules before you start. How completely do you want to go forward with this adventure? How far away are you willing to go? When do you have to be home?

- After choosing your letter, take a moment to brainstorm places and activities so you don't stand around for hours looking blankly into each other's eyes.

Over the Top

Invite other couples to go along with you. Let each couple choose a letter. Set a meeting place and a time. The couple that does the most things or finds the most places that correspond to their letter wins. For verification, have them snap a picture on their cell phone or camera at each stop.

2. Visit a Retro Roller Rink

Sure, it might conjure up images of junior high, with all the nervousness and sweaty palms that came with the "couples' skate," but good, old-

fashioned roller skating is not only fun, it's a great workout! Nowadays, many people have traded in their roller skates for the more modern, outdoor Rollerblades™, but for a fun (and heart-pounding) date idea, nothing beats the roller rink. Imagine it—the music, the sound of wheels on wood, skaters leaning into the turns and then picking up the pace on the straightaways. It's magical. And if you're lucky, you might even get to hold that special someone's hand under the disco ball.

 **Budget**

>$$ Most roller-skating rinks have inexpensive entrance fees, but you'll also need to cover refreshments and skate rentals—for two.

 **Steps to Success**

Have you forgotten how to roller skate, or never really learned? Here are easy, no-fail steps to get you moving around the rink in no time.

- Step 1: Place your feet in a "V" position, with your heels together and your toes apart.

- Step 2: Keep your body upright, and don't look down!

- Step 3: Bend your knees slightly and stretch your arms out for balance.

- Step 4: Begin to "march," not walk, using small baby steps. Lift your knees, keeping your feet in the "V" position.

- Step 5: Don't attempt to slide your skates. If your feet stay in the correct place, your skates will roll.

- Step 6: When you are ready for it, push your skate out to the side. This will get you moving forward.

If you are feeling ambitious, try skating backward—with the flow of traffic, of course. Skate just as you would going forward, except keep your toes together and your heels apart, in an inverse "V" position.

 ## Over the Top

- Buy your own roller skates, or buy a pair for your sweetie.

- Rent the roller-skating rink for the night for just the two of you. Provide the deejay with a CD of your date's favorite songs ahead of time. Be sure to include some fun and funky tunes, as well as some romantic ones to set the mood.

Get Connected

- To find a roller-skating rink in your area, check out *seskate.com/rinks*.

- Key search words: roller skate, rinks, how to skate

Nothing is sweeter than love,

Nothing is stronger,

Nothing higher,

Nothing wider,

Nothing more pleasant,

Nothing fuller nor better in
    heaven and earth.

THOMAS À KEMPIS

3. Pet Lover's Delight

What would this world be like without animals? Whether you prefer fur or feathers—or even scales!—it's impossible to deny the joy that pets bring to our lives.

Visiting a pet store with your date is a great way to get up close and personal with some cuddly creatures—and with each other. You may learn things you never knew before, like: Is she a dog lover? Does he have an "inner feline" just waiting to be released? And who between the two of you is really the most scared of creepy-crawly critters?

 Budget

$ Unless you're planning to make a purchase, visiting a pet store is free.

 Steps to Success

- Be sure to ask your date first if there is a particular animal that he or she is allergic to!

- Watch for handling instructions posted on the animal cages.

- Don't feed any animal without permission.

- Remember that a pet store is a place of business. Be considerate.

- Wash your hands thoroughly when you're finished.

Over the Top

- Make a date to volunteer to walk the dogs at a local animal shelter or humane society. You'll make some new furry friends, get some exercise, and have a whole lot of fun in the process.

- End the night watching your favorite animal movie.

Get Connected

Key search words: cats, dogs, pets, pet store, animal shelter, humane society

4. Sample Some Sushi

Sushi has been a staple of Japanese food for hundreds of years, but only recently in America has this culinary trend really taken hold. Many people wonder about the idea of eating bite-size pieces of raw fish on a dollop of rice. But not all sushi is raw—there are many "beginners' platters" that feature cooked fish or crabmeat. But if you're a novice, beware of the wasabi—a form of horseradish that usually comes on the side, legendary for its burning hot sensation in the nostrils if not diluted with soy sauce!

Sampling sushi with someone is a great way to try new things together. Even if you're already a die-hard fan, dare yourself to try something different—and dare your date to do the same!

Budget

$$$ Most sushi bars charge a la carte, and the price can add up quickly. If your budget is a concern, try ordering a sampler platter for a lower cost.

What to Take

- Chopsticks—learning to eat with them provides a great topic for conversation.

- An open mind

Over the Top

Try making your own sushi at home.
Working with raw fish can be tricky. Be sure
you have good instructions and follow them
carefully.

Get Connected

Key search words: sushi, make your own
sushi, Japanese restaurant and your state or
city

Love is love's reward.

JOHN DRYDEN

Strephon kissed me in the spring,
Robin in the fall,
But Colin only looked at me
And never kissed at all.

Strephon's kiss was lost in jest,
Robin's lost in play,
But the kiss in Colin's eyes
Haunts me night and day.

SARA TEASDALE

5. Take Me Out to the Ball Game

Nothing beats an evening of baseball. The satisfying sound of bat against ball. The pungent smell of popcorn. The glare of stadium lights. The voice of the announcer echoing through the stands. A gentle breeze blowing through your hair. Cotton candy, hot dogs, peanuts, soft drinks, and ice cream sundaes in plastic baseball caps. This sport is so much more than the final score.

Make a date to see your local team play. And make some noise. Baseball is an interactive sport. Shout, scream, boo, whistle, yell at the umpire, stomp your feet, clap your hands. Watch the scoreboard for names and stats.

Getting into the game will help you relax and enjoy your time together, without worrying about what to say or how to act.

Budget

$$ Ticket prices are generally pretty inexpensive for local games. If you watch though,

teams often have promotions where you can get in free or for a couple of bucks. Concessions are another story. You can easily spend a small fortune on food and drinks if you are not careful.

What to Take

- If you go to a day game, be sure you take sunglasses, sunscreen, and a cap. Also be sure to drink lots of water—the sun can be intense, and some seats aren't covered.

- If you go to a night game, take a light jacket. Even in the summer, the breeze high in the stands can get chilly.

Over the Top

Arrange for your date's name to appear on the JumboTron™ scoreboard. If the sentiment fits, add "I love you!" You will need to make arrangements for this in advance.

6. Antique Car Show

Cars and cars and more cars—all wearing a
polished shine you could see your face in. Beautiful,
bright red classics. Adorable little sports coupes.
Cars with fins. Cars with pinstripes. Cars with
colorful flames lapping at their sides. Music, lights,
and more excitement than you know what to do
with! What a great place to stage a date!

No matter what age group you and your date
fall into, this should be a satisfying event. Most
medium to large cities will have at least one show
a year. Next time you feel like doing something

different, see what your date has to say about exploring the health and well-being of the auto industry.

 Budget

$-$$ Car show ticket prices vary widely, so call ahead or check for the price online. Plan a few extra dollars for parking as well.

 What to Take

- Comfortable shoes

- Sunglasses, sunscreen, and a hat if the show is outside

- Camera—so you can take pictures of your date in front of some really classy numbers

Get Connected

Key search words: antique car shows followed by your city and state

Some people come into our lives and quickly go. Some stay for awhile and leave footprints on our hearts. And we are never, ever the same.

ANONYMOUS

7. Random Acts of Kindness

Who knew a selfless day of benevolent giving could be so compelling? Ask those who have tried it, and they will assure you it's something they want to do again and again. It really is true that when you're good to others, you're good to yourself. That translates easily to a truly satisfying date.

Tell your date ahead of time what you have in mind and begin looking for places to invest your acts of kindness. If you're paying attention, opportunities won't be difficult to find. Do you have an elderly neighbor who could use some help with their lawn? Or do you know someone who needs help painting their house? Check out your local chapter of Habitat for Humanity. Call your town's homeless shelter and find out how you can be of service. Ask a nursing home if you can visit the residents. Many of them may enjoy being read to or would like to have a letter written for them.

Need is not in short supply in our country, but it sometimes is pushed to the side. Such a date will give you both a better understanding of what really matters in life—and also a better understanding of the person you're dating.

Budget

$ Guaranteed—this one won't cost you a dime!

Steps to Success

- Don't just show up at the nursing home or shelter. Call ahead.

- Wear comfortable clothes and shoes.

- Leave your money and valuables at home.

- Put a smile on your face and keep it there no matter what you see or hear.

- Remember that this date is not about you.

Over the Top

Contact the Red Cross for information on natural disaster training. Together you can make a difference when people need help the most.

Get Connected

- Check out *volunteermatch.org* and *redcross.org*.

- If you are a nature lover, many zoos, state parks, and animal shelters need volunteers.

- Key search words: volunteer opportunities followed by your city and state

Many waters cannot quench love; rivers cannot wash it away. . . .

SONG OF SONGS 8:7

8. Eight Seconds!

Don't even think of climbing on one of those beasts. Leave that madness to the true cowboys. Rodeo is serious business! You can have a great time just watching from the stands and yelling your heads off as the riders attempt to stay up top for eight seconds—even though it seems like thirty minutes. The clowns are amazing. The lights, the earthy smell of the dirt in the arena, the excitement of the competition, and the whole outdoorsy nature of the event make it easy to get hooked. After just one date at the rodeo, you might find yourselves going back again and again. There just isn't anything else like it.

Budget

$ Rodeo tickets are typically quite reasonable—and so are the concessions.

What to Take

- Boots, if you have them. Rodeos are dirty, and there is plenty to step in.

- Hat (a cowboy hat if you have one)

- Wear jeans and a cotton shirt, if possible.

- Your best hootin' and hollerin' voice

- Binoculars

Steps to Success

- Rodeos are kind of a love-hate sort of thing. Don't spring it on your date. Make a few inquiries first.

- Unlike other shows, it might be a little smelly up close to the action. Find seats that are up high and far back from the arena.

- Treat your date to a barbeque dinner before the rodeo to get in the mood.

Over the Top

If you are brave and have the know-how, you both may want to enter as a contestant in a rodeo. Calf roping, barrel racing, and bronco riding are some of the events held in addition to bull riding. Make sure to cheer each other on and afterwards celebrate with a nice steak dinner.

Get Connected

Key words: rodeo followed by your town and state

Love consists in desiring to give what is our own to another and feeling his delight as our own.

EMANUEL SWEDENBORG

Romance Her

Rather than overwhelming
your date with a large bouquet of
flowers, send her one exquisite rose—or
take it along when you go to pick her up
for your date. A yellow rose symbolizes
friendship and caring. It's the perfect
innocent gift for a first date.

9. Night Golf

Who plays golf at night? So dark you can't tell your woods from your drivers! Okay, so nine holes is out of the question, but you should be able to see well

enough to do some putting on the green closest to the clubhouse. You'll do even better if you purchase a glow-in-the-dark golf ball. Yes, there really is such a thing.

This date is more about being together than improving your golf swing, but it really can be great fun. If all the courses in your area are posted with signs which say "Keep Out After Dark" or are locked up tight, try a driving range. Those are almost always open at night and you can have a great time with a basket or two of balls and a couple of drivers—all of which you can get right there at the range.

Budget

$ Night golf on an unrestricted, community course is literally free. Invest in a couple of those fancy glow-in-the-dark balls, borrow a couple of putters, and you're in business. A large basket of balls at the driving range is fairly inexpensive.

What to Take

- Light jacket
- Flashlight
- Golf balls and putters

Steps to Success

- Many driving ranges stay booked up and require reservations as much as a week in advance.
- Wear golf shoes or tennis shoes.

- Some golf courses would have no problem with your being there at night as long as you don't do any damage. However, it's best to call during business hours and ask if what you wish to do is permitted.

- Leave greens the way you found them.

Get Connected

Key search words: glow golf balls, golf course followed by your town and state

10. Play Laser Tag or Paintball

This is a great idea for a date and even more fun if you ask other couples to join you. Either way, the competition, the intrigue, the sneaking about, all add up to a top-notch event.

Laser tag is completely benign and appropriate for all ages. Paintball, on the other hand, is not for wimps. The paintball pellets actually sting, and it's messy. Experienced paintball players will tell you though—it's much more exciting than laser tag. Often played outdoors, there are many more

opportunities for strategy and role-playing.
Both laser tag and paintball offer an opportunity to
rescue and defend a certain female player or deliver
a romantic "you are my hero" kiss to a certain male
player.

 Budget

$$ Laser tag prices are reasonable. Paintball
prices may be higher if you have to pay extra
for supplies.

 What to Take

For paintball:

• Good shoes for running

• Mask

• Some type of head protection

- Cloth for cleaning your mask

- Bottled water

- Bug spray

Over the Top

Rent the paintball facility for your group exclusively. Afterwards, arrange to have a picnic on the property with all the fixings. Even if they don't provide food, they will probably allow you to bring your own.

Get Connected

Key search words: paintball, laser tag with your city and state, paintball or laser tag equipment

11. Experience an IMAX Theater

If you've never been to an IMAX theater, an
amazing treat awaits you and your date. It is truly
the ultimate movie experience. Theatergoers sit
on steeply rising rows of seats facing crystal clear
images on a screen eight stories high with wrap-
around digital surround sound. You literally feel
like you are part of the on-screen adventure, especially those that are viewed in 3D.

IMAX offers Hollywood classics as well as fabulous
adventure movies. You and your date can climb

Mt. Everest, experience the weightlessness of space, swim with great white sharks, or explore the Grand Canyon, all from the comfort and safety of your theater seats.

Or you can intertwine your fingers and let the tears flow freely while you enjoy a wonderfully romantic tearjerker like *Casablanca* or *Love Story*.

Budget

$$ Prices run slightly higher than the prices of regular theater tickets. Tickets may include access to interesting exhibits and attractions in proximity to the theater.

Steps to Success

- Be prepared for intense light and sound. For some, this translates to motion sickness and loss of equilibrium. You might want to ask your date about certain sensitivities before pursuing this activity.

- Those who know say the best place to sit in an IMAX theater is "center back" due to the size of the theater seating in relationship to the size of the screen.

Over the Top

Have a private showing at an IMAX theater for just you and your date or invite all your friends and make it a party.

Get Connected

Check out *imax.com* for theater locations in your area, upcoming films, and specific fees.

12. Indoor Rock Climbing

This may seem like an extreme date, but it really isn't. Even children can manage this sport with proper instruction. You will both need to be in good physical condition, however.

Spend some time together preparing for this exciting event, studying technique online. By the time you arrive, you and

your date will be completely hyped and ready to take on your challenge. Climb side by side or one behind the other so you can encourage and cheer each other on. On your way home, stop someplace where you can spend some time discussing how truly strong, brave, and amazing you both are while sipping a nutrition-conscious fruit smoothie or a hot cup of green tea.

 **Budget**

$$ Prices vary from gym to gym. Be sure to ask if equipment rental and training is included.

What to Take

- Comfortable, loose-fitting clothing that allows you a full range of motion, such as T-shirts, shorts, sweatpants, or leggings

- A sweatshirt to keep you warm when you aren't climbing

- Shoes should have rubber soles with a good grip and fit as tightly as possible on your feet.

Over the Top

Rent a mobile rock-climbing wall and have a party in the backyard! Invite other couples and have some fun. After working up an appetite, fire up the grill.

Get Connected

- At *indoorclimbing.com* you can locate a facility in your area. A climbing simulator is also available to help you enhance your skills. You can find out how to tailor your physical fitness program in preparation for rock-climbing training. And you can find out what equipment is required and where you can purchase or rent it.

- Key search words: rent a rock-climbing wall followed by your city and state

The greatest pleasure of life is love.

SIR WILLIAM TEMPLE

First Love

I ne'er was struck before that hour
With love so sudden and so sweet,
Her face it bloomed like a sweet
   flower
And stole my heart away complete.

I never saw so sweet a face
As that I stood before.
My heart has left its dwelling place
And can return no more.

JOHN CLARE

13. Renaissance Faire

Ribbons and flags wave in the wind. People in the colorful costumes of a bygone era are all around you. Everywhere you turn you hear bells, lutes, and lilting foreign accents. You feel intoxicated by the smell of exotic foods and flowers. You're probably at a Renaissance Faire!

Part craft fair, part historical reenactment, part performance art, these delightful journeys into the Elizabethan era are great fun and relatively easy to find almost anywhere in the country. You'll find booths selling crafts and food; parades winding their way through the crowds; jugglers, musicians, and other entertainers performing right out in the open. Everywhere you look, you will find excitement and entertainment.

Budget

$-$$ Ticket prices are usually reasonable. Expect to pay extra for food and parking.

Over the Top

- Go online and find specifics of the Elizabethan era, including dress and social etiquette. Attend the faire in costume and act the part.

Get Connected

- Go to *renfaire.com* for listings and specifics such as dates and pricing.

- Key search words: renaissance faires

Blessed is the influence of one true, loving human soul on another.

GEORGE ELIOT

14. Tour a Local Factory

Imagine yourself in Willy Wonka's chocolate factory taking a dip in a chocolate river or having your taste buds tantalized by a melt-in-your-mouth treat. Maybe you can't do that, but you can see real-life places where your favorite treats are made. Many factories have opened their doors to the public. Some have gift stores and, most exciting, some even offer free samples. Whatever your fancy, whether it be edible treats or pottery or toys, most areas in the country boast a factory or two. Many provide guest tours which can be both entertaining and educational. Some even offer exciting interactive exhibits such as the Boeing jet plant in the state of Washington.

Ask your date for a short list of his or her favorite things and see what you can find in your area that would make you both shiver with anticipation.

 **Budget**

$ Typically, companies do not charge for a tour of their facilities. They are proud to show you around. Exceptions are companies that are espionage sensitive, such as fashion and technology producers.

Steps to Success

- Wear comfortable shoes and a light sweater or jacket you can take off. Some plants are very warm, others icy.

- Leave what you don't need in the car. You'll want your hands free to grab free samples.

- Many companies will not allow you to take photos. Be sure to ask.

Get Connected

Key search words: factories, factory tours followed by your city and state

15. Drive-In Movie Theater

A fun alternative to the traditional dinner-and-a-movie date is the drive-in theater. While perhaps not as popular as in their glory days, drive-ins have been making a comeback in the last few years, and at least one of these hidden treasures can be found in most cities. They boast huge screens, and many have updated sound systems that broadcast over your radio. Some drive-ins will show two or even three movies for one admission, so you can stay for as many as you'd like. A night spent under the stars at the drive-in is so much more than just watching a movie—it's a fun, nostalgic, romantic experience you'll not soon forget.

Budget

$$ Most drive-in admissions are comparable to or less than a regular theater, but remember to take some extra cash for the snack bar.

 What to Take

- You can pack your own snacks and drinks or plan on visiting the snack bar. If you're planning on staying for more than one feature, you may even want to take along something for dinner that can be eaten easily in the car.

- Blankets and pillows so you can get comfortable, especially if it's chilly out

 Over the Top

Get online and find some drive-ins that sound especially fun or historically significant. Then get some other couples onboard and plan a fun road trip to visit these theaters. You can keep the cost down by having all the girls share one hotel room and the guys share another. Find interesting, historic places to eat and sleep along the way.

Get Connected

- Check out *driveinmovie.com* or *driveintheater.com* for up-to-date listings and descriptions of operating drive-ins in each state.

- Key search words: drive-in movie followed by your city and state

16. Go Fishing

Fishing is a lot more than sitting on the bank with a cane pole—though that could be a lovely date as well. It's an exciting sport and one that would make a genuinely entertaining date. Just imagine yourself catching the "big one!"

If you don't have the equipment to go fishing, it's easy to find at your local sporting goods store. Take your date along. Choosing lures is a very personal activity. If you want live bait, you can usually find it at a bait store located conveniently near the lake.

Rent a boat or just cast from the shore. It won't take more than a few minutes to get the hang of it. Chat away or simply be quiet together. Feel the sun on your face and the breeze in your hair. Focus on each cast, and then share the experience with each other over a picnic lunch. If you actually catch a fish—well, that's just icing on the cake.

 **Budget**

$$ If you already have equipment or can borrow some, you'll be way ahead. You'll both need a fishing license, which can be purchased almost anywhere—hardware stores, bait and tackle shops, any store that has a fishing department.

What to Take

- Fishing rods and tackle

- Bottled water

- Lunch

- Hat

- Sunscreen

- Wet wipes

- Jacket

- Comfortable shoes with rubber soles

- Net and bucket

 Over the Top

- Hire a fishing guide and see how many you can catch!

- The winner must buy lunch at a fancy seafood restaurant.

Get Connected

- Be sure to ask the locals where the best fishing is.

- Key search words: fishing, fishing lures, fishing guides

Greet one another
with a kiss of love.

1 Peter 5:14

Romance Him

Dress to please your special
someone. Forget about trendy outfits
and the newest fads. If he compliments
what you're wearing, wear it again.
If he seems to like less makeup—cut back
on the lipstick and eye shadow. If he likes
long hair, let yours down when you're out
with him. In this way, you show him
that you respect his taste and want
to be pleasing to him.

17. Attend a Madrigal Dinner

A Madrigal Dinner is a step back into the Middle Ages. Singers dressed in sixteenth-century English costumes announce the arrival of the Christmas season with a concert of traditional carols. Then actors dressed as the king and queen and their royal court join the singers on stage.

The guests are seated at tables lavishly decorated in Christmas finery, waiting to be served a dinner consisting of traditional Christmas period fare: wassail (hot apple cider), boar's head (prime rib), and figgie pudding (bread pudding). Between courses, actors perform scenes from a play written entirely in rhyme and seasoned with the Christmas message. The audience is often invited to interact with the actors either as members of the royal court or guests at a royal event, such as a wedding. The theme is lighthearted and romantic, reminiscent of the King Arthur legends, and often revolves around the marriage of a prince or princess, making it a special date for the holidays.

 **Budget**

> $$ Madrigal dinners are most often pre-sented by school or church groups. An affordable fee is charged to cover the cost of the meal, costumes, and props.

Over the Top

Go dressed in period costumes or sign up to be part of the production. Each rehearsal you attend becomes an additional date.

Get Connected

Key search words: madrigal dinner

Love without friendship is like a house without a foundation.

DAVID VALENTINE

18. Prepare a Dinner Together

Making a meal together is a perfect way to get to know each other better while exploring your own culinary talents. You'll find out about each other's likes and dislikes and have fun gleaning information from each other's experience in the kitchen—or have a good-hearted laugh at the lack of it. Plan a dinner around a theme and decorate the dining room. For example, if your theme is Mexican food, deck out the room with a fun tablecloth, chili pepper lights, and a piñata. Or you could don chef hats and aprons and take turns putting on a cooking show for each other as if you're the next Food Network stars. And the best part is, after you're finished, you can sit down, relax, and enjoy the fruit of your labor.

 Budget

$-$$ Cost will depend greatly on your dinner selection—whether simple or fancy.

 What to Take

- Make sure you have the pans and utensils necessary for the recipe.

- Agree on a menu and do your shopping ahead of time.

Steps to Success

Keep it lighthearted. If your finished product is inedible, you've still had fun and created a memory, and you can always order a pizza!

Over the Top

- Prepare a full five-course meal. Do as much of the preparation as you can together, then hire someone or ask a friend to come and put the finishing touches on the meal and serve it. Adorn the table nicely and have soft music playing. Dress up as if you were going to dinner at a five-star restaurant.

- Take a cooking class together. Most cities offer classes ranging from haute cuisine to down-home fare.

Get Connected

- Check out *recipesource.com* and *allrecipes.com* for menu ideas.

- Key search words: recipes, HGTV, cooking class followed by your city and state

Love is like the wild rose-briar,
Friendship like the holly-tree—
The holly is dark when the rose-briar blooms
But which will bloom most constantly?

EMILY BRONTË

19. Snow Date

Remember when you were a child and it snowed,
you opened your mouth and caught snowflakes on
your tongue? Why not do it again. And what could
be more romantic than freshly fallen snow? Make
the most of this wintertime delight by enjoying its
invigorating charms with your sweetheart. Bundle
up and head outdoors for a scenic walk. Make
snow angels and have a snow fight along the way.
Or, for the more adventurous, go snow tubing,
sledding, or even snowshoeing. Whatever activity
you choose, let your inner child come out, have

fun, and don't be afraid to get a little icy. Finish off your date with a cup of hot chocolate topped with marshmallows enjoyed in front of a cozy fire as you share fond memories of playing in the snow as a child.

Budget

$ This date can be arranged with little or no money. The only expenses beyond the hot chocolate would be buying or renting a sled, snow tube, or snowshoes.

What to Take

- Hats, scarves, gloves, earmuffs, a coat, and lots of layers of clothing to keep you warm

- Any snow gear you may have on hand

Over the Top

- If there's an outdoor ice-skating rink in your area, include it in your date.

- Enjoy a fondue dinner or some other favorite, warm comfort food along with your hot chocolate.

Get Connected

- If budget is an issue, try checking *ebay.com* for quality used snow toys.

- Key search words: snowshoes, snow sleds, snow tubes

There is no remedy for love, but to love more.

Henry David Thoreau

20. Engage in a Friendly Competition

Who's the most competitive? Do either of you have any hidden talents the other doesn't know about? A little friendly competition can provide a fun way to spend time together, and you just may discover something new about each other along the way. Pick something that you both enjoy doing, or maybe something you've never, or only rarely, tried before. You could go bowling, play pool or miniature golf, or take a swing at the batting cages.

You may even want to make it more interesting by agreeing on a prize for the winner—such as the loser treats the winner to dessert or the winner gets to pick the next movie you see together. Or, purchase a trophy or other small memento of your evening to go to the winner. You could even agree to pass it back and forth to the winner on future dates.

Budget

$ Most of these activities are relatively inexpensive and can provide hours of fun.

Steps to Success

- If you tend to be very competitive, make sure you keep it lighthearted and don't get

so caught up in the game that you forget
your main goal of having fun together.

- Have fun laughing with each other, but
  make sure it's all in good fun (for both of
  you) and that you steer clear of anything
  that could be hurtful.

- Cheer each other on and celebrate one
  another's successes.

 Over the Top

Join a local team or league together and
make it a regular event.

 Get Connected

Key search words: miniature golf, bowling,
billiards, trophies

My Love, My Life

What greater thing is there for
   two human souls

than to feel that they are joined for life,

to strengthen each other in all labor,

to rest on each other in all sorrow,

to minister to each other in all pain,

to be one with each other

in silent, unspeakable memories

at the moment of the last parting.

GEORGE ELIOT

21. Picnic in the Park

When sunshine and pleasant weather beckon, prepare a picnic basket and a small cooler for drinks, grab your sweetheart, and head outdoors. Find a scenic park nearby and enjoy a peaceful afternoon. Walk hand in hand, feed the ducks, and join in the fun on the playground. See how high you can fly on the swings, slide down the sliding board, or pair up on the teeter-totter. Lie on your backs on the blanket and describe what you see in the clouds. Read a book or magazine out loud. Then enjoy a relaxing picnic and bask in the sunlight and the beauty of nature.

Budget

$ All you should need to buy is food and drinks for a picnic.

What to Take

- A picnic: For a romantic meal, pack up some crackers, cheeses, lunchmeats, fruit, dessert, and sparkling grape juice. Or if this date is more spontaneous, just pick up some sandwiches and chips along the way.

- A picnic blanket

- Some extra bread to feed the ducks or nuts for the squirrels

- A card game or checkers set

- If you both like to read, take along a book of poetry or other literature and take turns reading to each other.

Over the Top

Choose a safe park and ask your sweetheart to meet you there at dusk. Have a white-tablecloth, candlelit dinner set up at a picnic table awaiting his or her arrival.

Get Connected

- Most cities list the area parks and their features on the city's website.

- Check out *picnicfun.com* for cool picnic accessories.

- Key search words: picnic foods, picnic basket

22. Celebrate the Holidays in Style

Holidays provide great opportunities to get out of a rut and try something different. On Easter, go

to a sunrise service. On the Fourth of July, attend a parade or find a great place to watch fireworks. On Halloween, throw a costume party or volunteer to man a booth together at your church's harvest festival. Go to a candlelight service or midnight mass on Christmas Eve. Be sure to check your local paper for upcoming events in your area, and make the most of the holidays as you enjoy them together.

Budget

$ Of course, prices will vary depending on what you choose to do, but many holiday activities are free.

Over the Top

- At Christmastime, attend a local

performance of Handel's *Messiah, The Nutcracker* ballet, or Charles Dickens' classic *A Christmas Carol*.

- On Easter, plan an Easter egg hunt for two. Fill some plastic eggs with small gifts and love notes for each other. Then have fun hiding and searching for them.

- Take a limousine, helicopter, or horse-drawn carriage ride to see the Christmas lights.

Get Connected

- Type in the name of your city followed by the word *events* to find listings of upcoming events in your area.

- Key search words: Valentine's Day, St. Patrick's Day, Easter, Fourth of July, Halloween, Thanksgiving, Christmas, holidays, calendar of events

23. Trash or Treasure?

You've probably heard the old adage, "One man's trash is another man's treasure." Why not see if this idea rings true for the two of you? Visit some yard or estate sales or go to a flea market, thrift store, or antique shop together. Have fun finding unusual items or things that bring back special memories for you. While you're there, have a contest to see who can find the ugliest or most unusual item. You may even want to purchase your finds as a gift for each other and a fun memento of your date.

 **Budget**

$-$$ This date should be fairly inexpensive—unless, of course, you find lots of "treasures" you just can't leave behind.

 Over the Top

- Look for an item you think may be priced well below its value; then try selling it online. If you make a profit, celebrate over dinner at a fancy restaurant or some other activity you normally wouldn't treat yourselves to.

- Look up some unusual items online or think of your favorite childhood toys that aren't around anymore. Make a list beforehand, and then go on a scavenger hunt to see how many of these items you can find at sales or stores in your area.

Get Connected

- Many newspapers have online listings of yard sales in the area. Type in the name of the paper, then look under the "classifieds" section.

- Key search words: antiques, thrift store, flea market, yard sale, garage sale

A friend is one
who knows you and loves you
just the same.

ELBERT HUBBARD

24. Visit a Botanical Garden or Garden Show

There's something romantic about being surrounded by beautiful flowers, trees, and ornamental plants. Enjoy walking hand in hand and admiring the wonders of nature artistically displayed at a botanical garden. While this activity is a great choice for a nice, sunny day, many gardens also feature large greenhouse areas that can be enjoyed year-round.

Another fun option is to attend a garden show. Some shows include a variety of plants, while others feature a certain type of plant, such as roses or bonsai trees. And many include demonstrations and classes so you can learn more about planting and growing these items yourself. You may even wish to purchase a plant for your sweetheart and enjoy planting and taking care of it together.

 Budget

$-$$ There is usually a modest entry fee for botanical gardens or garden shows. Take extra money in case you want to make a purchase.

 What to Take

Take along a picnic to enjoy on the grounds. (Call beforehand to make sure picnicking is permitted.)

Over the Top

- Invite another couple or two on a road trip to visit several gardens. Choose a major garden, such as the New York Botanical Gardens, as your final destination. You can keep the cost down by having all the girls share a room and the guys share another.

- Grow a bonsai tree together. For information, check out *bonsaigardener.com*.

Get Connected

- *Wikipedia.com* provides a comprehensive list of botanical gardens in each state. Go to the website and type in "list of botanical gardens in the United States."

- Key search words: botanical gardens, garden show, rose show, bonsai show

A Kiss

And what is a kiss, when all is done?
A promise given under seal—a vow
A signature acknowledged—a rosy dot
Over the i of Loving—a secret whispered
To listening lips apart—a moment made
Immortal, with a rush of wings unseen—
A sacrament of blossoms, a new song
Sung by two hearts to an old simple tune—
The ring of one horizon around two souls
Together, all alone!

EDMOND ROSTAND

25. Take a Hike!

Instead of telling each other to "take a hike," take one together. Plan a day trip to a state or national park and explore the hiking trails. You might want to stop at the park office or visitor center on your way in and pick up a map. Choose a trail that fits

your level of fitness and experience and head out for an adventure. Keep your ears tuned in and your eyes open for interesting birds and other wildlife; and take time to notice details along the way, such as pretty wildflowers, ferns, moss, and insects.

Budget

$ Some parks charge a small day-use fee, but many allow you to explore free of charge.

What to Take

- A backpack, layered clothing, and comfortable shoes
- Plenty of bottled water
- Trail mix and/or energy bars
- Binoculars

- A compass

- If there are any caves you want to explore along the trail, you'll need a flashlight. Check your map to make sure the cave isn't off limits to visitors.

- A small first-aid kit

- Cell phone or GPS device

WOW Over the Top

- For the really adventurous (experienced hikers only, please!), some parks offer heli-hiking expeditions in which you're flown by helicopter to a certain destination. You then hike your way back to a pickup spot. You'll need to make sure you're physically ready and have the right gear for this adventure.

- Take a rock-climbing course together. Then plan some day-trips to try out your skills.

Get Connected

- Go to *nps.gov* to find a complete listing of national parks. State parks can be found by searching for the name of the state followed by the words *state parks*.

- Key search words: hiking, hiking trails, bird watching

Let no one who loves be called unhappy. Even love unreturned has its rainbow.

J. M. BARRIE

26. Go Horseback Riding

Whether you're an expert equestrian or your last and only horseback-riding experience was the pony ride at the state fair, an afternoon at the riding stables can be an exciting, romantic adventure. If you're new to horseback riding, most riding stables will give you a short prep course about how to handle the horses and provide guided expeditions if you're uncomfortable going out on your own. They also try to match the horse's temperament with your level of experience. So saddle up and hit the trail for a great new adventure with the one you love.

 **Budget**

$$ Fees will vary from stable to stable and may depend partly on how scenic the trail is. Make sure the stable you choose stresses safety and offers a good introductory course.

 What to Take

- Comfortable clothing that covers your arms and legs

- Heavy shoes or boots

- A hat

- Insect repellent

- A jacket

 Over the Top

- Go on a special "themed" expedition. Some stables offer rides that include a campfire meal and/or entertainment. Others will let you get a taste of what it would be like to work on a ranch, rounding up cattle.

- If you're near the ocean, go horseback riding on the beach.

- If you can time your ride around sunrise or sunset, it's a special treat!

Get Connected

Key search words: horseback riding, riding stables, horseback riding on the beach, horseback ride with meal

27. Get Literary

Explore your intellectual side. Even if you're not an avid reader, you might be surprised at the conversations a visit to a bookstore, library, or book fair can spark. Browse the shelves and talk about anything that draws your attention. If you're not in the habit of reading, find a book about something that interests you—a sport or hobby or something you've wanted to learn more about. It might be fun to visit the children's section and both try to find your favorite childhood bedtime story.

If you are in the market for a good read or just enjoy the thrill of the hunt, a used-book store or book fair is a great choice. From early editions of literary classics to collectors' editions of your favorite comic books, you're sure to find something that interests you, and often at surprisingly reasonable prices.

 **Budget**

$ Browsing a library or bookstore is free, but take along a little money in case you decide to visit the coffee bar. Libraries also have regular used-book sales that might offer something of interest.

Over the Top

Form a private book club for two. Choose a book. (You may want to purchase or check out a copy for each of you.) Read it separately; then talk about it over dessert at a coffee shop or café. If one of you isn't a reader, get the book on tape from your local library.

Get Connected

Key search words: bookstore, library, book club books

28. Have a Zoolighful Date

You may think of the zoo as a place for kids (or people who have kids), but it can provide a fun day of entertainment for anyone. Many zoos allow visitors to feed certain animals in interactive exhibits, and most zoos have live animal demonstrations or shows daily. In addition to the animals, which provide new and different entertainment every time you visit, many zoos also host some beautiful landscaping and gardens, making them great places to walk and talk while getting some fresh air.

There are also many wildlife sanctuaries which are usually privately owned and funded. These refuges take in abused and neglected animals. They usually don't have fancy facilities but can sometimes offer a more "up-close and personal" experience with the animals than you would find at a zoo.

Go ahead—take a walk on the wild side with the stars of the animal kingdom.

Budget

$-$$ Most zoos have reasonable admission prices. Take a little extra for the snack bar, train rides, and souvenirs.

What to Take

- Most zoos will allow you to take along a picnic, or you can plan to eat at the snack bar.

- Sunglasses and sunscreen

- Binoculars could help you see animals you might otherwise miss.

- Comfortable shoes and clothes

- Camera

Over the Top

- Have fun trying to identify which type of animal each of you most resembles based on appearance, personality traits, etc. Take pictures of each other with the chosen animals. Choose carefully; you could get yourself into trouble!

- Some zoos host special benefit dinners, dances, or concerts on their grounds. Make plans to attend one of these special events.

- Take a behind-the-scenes tour with a zoo-keeper. These can be expensive and need to be booked well in advance.

 Get Connected

- On *aza.com*, you can find a zoo in your area that is accredited by the Association of Zoos and Aquariums. In order to be accredited, a zoo must meet high standards of commitment to conservation, humane treatment of animals, and provide habitats that mimic the animals' natural environments as closely as possible.

- Key search words: wildlife refuge or wildlife sanctuary followed by your city and state

At the touch of love everyone becomes a poet.

PLATO

Romance Her ♥

Treat her to a fancy dinner under
the stars. You will need a card table, two
chairs, a white tablecloth and napkins, china
plates, goblets, silverware, a vase of flowers,
candles in candlesticks, and the best take-out
food you can afford. Take care to research
your location. She'll be dazzled!

29. How Puzzling!

Pick out a jigsaw puzzle to complete together. Unless you're a real puzzle enthusiast, find something that's challenging but can be completed in an evening or two. Put on some music, grab some snacks, and enjoy a relaxing evening of puzzle solving and conversation. When you're finished, you'll have the satisfaction of working as a team to complete something. You could also glue your masterpiece together, frame it, and hang it on the wall as a reminder of the great time you had putting it together.

Budget

$-$$ You'll need a puzzle, some puzzle glue, and a frame (if you choose to display your puzzle afterward), and some snack foods and drinks.

Steps to Success

- Agree on the rules before you begin. Is peeking at the picture on the box allowed?

- The edges are a good place to start.

- If you get stuck, change places to gain a fresh perspective.

- Put the last piece into place together!

Over the Top

Have a photo puzzle made from a picture of the two of you or from a picture that's meaningful to both of you. Many photo development labs offer this service, or you can order a photo puzzle online.

Get Connected

Key search words: jigsaw puzzles, photo puzzle

Love is
the expansion of two
natures in such fashion that
each includes the other, each is
enriched by the other.

FELIX ADLER

30. Hit the Deck

For a marine adventure you'll always remember, rent a sailboat, pontoon boat, or paddleboat and head out on the lake for a day of fun in the sun. If there are several marinas on the lake, you could plan to dock and explore other areas along the way. Or, if you live near one, take a ferry ride and explore the sights when you reach your destination. Keep an eye out for birds, fish, turtles, and other wildlife along the way. You never know what new sights you may see.

Budget

$-$$$ The amount you spend will vary greatly depending on which activity you choose. If budget is a concern, a paddleboat may be the vessel of choice.

What to Take

- Be sure to take sunscreen and sunglasses.

- Wear comfortable shoes that don't get slick when wet.

- You may want a light jacket since temperatures tend to be lower and winds stronger over water.

- If you'll be out for a while, take a picnic lunch or some snacks and drinks.

Over the Top

- Make arrangements to arrive a little early and deck the boat out with flowers and other simple decorations. Hide a small token of your affection or love notes somewhere onboard for your sweetheart to discover along the way.

- If you live near the coast, take a day cruise. Although the boats used are smaller than the big cruise liners, they still offer many of the amenities, including swimming pools, restaurants, and shows.

Get Connected

- Many state parks offer boat rentals and provide information on their websites.

- Key search words: boat rentals, sailboat rentals, paddleboats, ferry rides, day cruises

31. Fun at the Beach

If you live near the coast, the beach is the perfect place to spend a day with the one you love. Have a picnic on the beach. Wade along the shore, walking hand in hand. Build a sand castle together. Watch

the sun set over the ocean, observing all the beautiful changes in color.

If you're landlocked, this date may take a little more creativity and imagination, but it can still be lots of fun. Take a picnic to a park that has a large sandbox area. Kick off your shoes and play tag in the sand. Build a sand castle. You could even take a couple of seashells with you, relax on your picnic blanket, and "listen to the ocean" by playing a CD of ocean sounds or by placing the seashell up to your ear. Close your eyes and imagine your dream vacation at the beach. Describe what you see to each other.

Budget

$ This is an inexpensive date that can provide hours of entertainment.

What to Take

- A picnic and picnic blanket

- Sunglasses and sunscreen

- Binoculars to look for aquatic life at the beach

- Comfortable shoes that you don't mind getting sandy

- A light jacket

Over the Top

- If you're nowhere near a beach, plan a trip to one. Maybe one of you has relatives who live near the coast and would enjoy your visit.

- If you live near the beach and go often, try something you normally don't do. Visit the boardwalk or an old coastal town as if you were a tourist.

Get Connected

- National seashores provide beautiful stretches of natural beaches to explore. Since they are protected, they aren't over-developed with hotels and resorts. You can find a list of them by going to *nps.gov* and doing a search for national seashores.

- If you're looking for a local park with sand, try a search for the name of your city followed by the word *parks*.

- Key search words: beach, seashore, boardwalk, seashells

32. Night at the Opera

Whether you or your loved one is a connoisseur of fine operatic music or this is your first experience with the genre, an evening at the opera is an enriching experience to share. Enjoy dressing up for the occasion, and plan to dine at a nice restaurant either before or after the show. Since many operas are performed in a foreign language, it's a good idea to educate yourself beforehand on the basic plot of the story. It also helps to arrive a little early so you have plenty of time to find your seats and read over the program, which will summarize the plot for you and give you information about the performers. The more you know beforehand, the easier it will be for you to understand and enjoy the production.

Budget

$$-$$$ Ticket prices will vary depending upon the location of your seats. Be sure to order your tickets several weeks in advance. If budget is a concern, find a local college that puts on operatic productions.

Steps to Success

- Keep an open mind. If you've never attended an opera before, try not to form an opinion before you try it.

- If you have trouble following the plot, don't put too much pressure on yourself.

Focus instead on the skillfulness of the performers and the artistry of the scenery.

Over the Top

- Purchase box seats for an especially memorable evening.

- Purchase some decorative opera glasses and have them engraved. Present them to your loved one as a lasting memento of the first opera you saw together.

Get Connected

- Google the name of the opera you will be attending to find a plethora of information about it.

- Key search words: opera followed by your city and state

How Do I Love Thee?

How do I love thee? Let me count the ways.
I love thee to the depth and breadth and height
My soul can reach, when feeling out of sight
For the ends of Being and ideal Grace.
I love thee to the level of every day's
Most quiet need, by sun and candle-light.

ELIZABETH BARRETT BROWNING

33. Go to the Fair

A county or state fair can provide something out of the ordinary to do on a date. Besides the rides and carnival games, most fairs also offer free concerts and other entertainment. You could explore your love of animals in the livestock arena and petting barn or take a look at some local artwork. See the latest and greatest in automobiles and gadgets. Of course, you can't go to the fair without sampling some fair food. Have some of your old favorites—corn dogs, turkey legs, cotton candy, funnel cakes—or try something new, like fried mashed potatoes on a stick, apple fries, or chocolate-covered cheesecake. You could even speculate about what next year's new fried food on a stick might be!

Budget

$-$$ The cost of rides, games, and food at the fair can add up quickly, so if budget is a concern, take advantage of the free events and exhibits that are included in your admission.

Over the Top

Plan several months in advance to grow or make something together and enter it in the fair. Categories range from amateur photography to robotics, from baking to vegetable gardening. You should be able to find details about categories, as well as entry rules and deadlines, on the fair's website.

Get Connected

- Most fairs will have a website where you can find pertinent information.

- Key search words: the name of your county or state followed by county/state fair

Gravitation cannot be held responsible for people falling in love.

ALBERT EINSTEIN

34. We All Scream for Ice Cream!

Nothing beats a bowl of rich, creamy homemade ice cream on a hot summer day. And what better way to work up an appetite and have a great time

in the process than to churn it yourself. Purchase or borrow an old-fashioned, hand-cranked ice-cream maker; then head to the grocery store to get the ingredients and your favorite toppings. Don't forget the ice and rock salt. Mix up your confectionary treat together, and then take turns churning it into a frozen delight. Finally, make your own sundaes, kick back, and enjoy the fruit of your labor.

Budget

$ This date is fairly inexpensive, especially if you already have or can borrow an ice-cream maker.

Over the Top

Before your loved one arrives, decorate your
dining room like an old-fashioned ice-cream
parlor, complete with soda glasses, a fun
tablecloth, straws in an antique-looking
straw holder, and so forth. Play a CD of
oldies in the background.

 ## Get Connected

Key search words: homemade ice-cream
recipes, sundae toppings

35. He Flies through the Air with the Greatest of Ease

Who is he? The daring young man on the flying trapeze, of course! When is the last time you went to the circus? Find out when the next one is coming your way and grab your sweetheart for an evening of three-ring excitement. Take a little trip down memory lane as you watch the circus stars perform daring acts and unbelievable stunts. Enjoy the funny antics of the clowns. And don't forget to enjoy some old favorites while you're there, like peanuts, popcorn, and cotton candy.

Budget

$$ Ticket prices vary according to location in the arena. Take along a little extra for snacks and perhaps a souvenir.

Over the Top

Some circuses offer special VIP tickets, which entitle the holder to prime seating as well as a moment in the spotlight, participating in the performance. They also sometimes offer a preshow for those arriving early, during which you can meet the performers and enjoy some behind-the-scenes activities.

Get Connected

Key search words: circus, animal-free circuses

What Is Love?

Love is patient, love is kind. It
does not envy, it does not boast,
it is not proud. It is not rude, it
is not self-seeking, it is not easily
angered, it keeps no record of
wrongs. Love does not delight in
evil but rejoices with the truth.
It always protects, always trusts,
always hopes, always perseveres.
Love never fails.

I Corinthians 13:4-8

36. Make Pizza from Scratch

Visit the grocery store together and pick out ingredients and toppings for your pizza. Go with your favorites or throw in something unusual. Don't forget the sauce. Or if you're really ambitious, try making your own. Have fun kneading the dough and trying to toss it in the air like they do on TV. (You may want to make extra dough to allow for some mishaps!) Agree on toppings for a larger pizza, or make several smaller pizzas so you can try different combinations.

Budget

$ Since you'll be doing the cooking your-selves, cost should be minimal.

Steps to Success

• Make sure you have all the necessary cooking utensils on hand before you begin: pizza pans, pizza cutter, etc.

• Find a recipe for the dough and/or sauce ahead of time. If you want to save time, you can buy a dough mix or use flatbread as your crust.

Over the Top

For an added touch, find some Italian music to play in the background. Create ambiance by adorning the table with a red-and-white checkered tablecloth and adding flowers in a decorative bottle.

Get Connected

Key search words: pizza recipes, pizza toppings

The most precious possession that ever comes to a man in this world is a woman's heart.

JOSIAH G. HOLLAND

37. Learn a Foreign Language

Is there a language you or your loved one is interested in learning? If so, why not have fun spending time learning together and stretch your mind and your vocabulary in the process? Most community colleges offer courses in several different foreign languages. Find one that interests you, and take it together. Practice speaking to each other in the foreign language on a regular basis as you learn new phrases. When you finish the course, celebrate by visiting a local authentic restaurant that specializes in the culture of the language you're studying and try out your vocabulary skills.

Budget

$$-$$$ College courses can be rather expensive. However, many community colleges offer noncredit personal enrichment courses at a lower cost than traditional classes.

Steps to Success

- Don't be too competitive about your progress in the class. Instead, help and encourage each other.

- If you don't catch on right away, don't get discouraged. Be proud of yourself for tackling something new and for choosing to learn just for fun.

Over the Top

Make plans to visit a country on a mission trip with your church where the language you've learned is the native language.

Get Connected

Key search words: foreign language courses, community college, junior college, personal enrichment courses

The consciousness of loving and being loved brings a warmth and a richness to life that nothing else can bring.

OSCAR WILDE

38. Visit an Aquarium

Is there an aquarium nearby? If so, get your loved one and dive on in for an exciting glimpse of what life is like under the sea. You'll see everything from

aquatic life that's native to your area to deep-sea creatures that look like something out of a science fiction movie. There's lots of scope for the imagination, as well as the freedom to walk and talk at your own pace. And, since many aquatic exhibits are housed indoors, a trip to the aquarium makes a perfect rainy-day activity.

 **Budget**

> $$ Admission prices vary based on location. You may want to consider investing in a season or annual pass.

 **Over the Top**

> Visit a SeaWorld Adventure Park. In addition to attractions you might find at

other aquariums, they offer rides, shows, and waterside dining. You can also purchase tickets to one of their behind-the-scenes tours in which you're allowed to interact or even swim with the sea animals.

Get Connected

- For a list of public aquariums worldwide, go to *aquae.com*.

- For more information about SeaWorld, visit *seaworld.com*.

- Key search words: aquarium followed by your city and state

39. The Play's the Thing!

To add a little dramatic flair to your dating repertoire, take your loved one to a play or musical production. You could opt to see a professional production at the performing arts center in your city, or you may want to check out the local talent of a community theater group, attend a high school or college production, or visit a small theater that showcases the works of local playwrights. You could also check to see if there is an upcoming Shakespearean Festival or Shakespeare in the Park event in your area. Whatever your choice, you're sure to enjoy the mystery, make-believe, and magic of the stage.

Budget

$-$$ You'll find a wide range of ticket prices depending on what production you choose to attend.

Over the Top

If going to a play awakens the thespian in you both, consider joining a local theater group together or trying out for small parts in a play.

Get Connected

- For a comprehensive listing of plays, both modern and classic, as well as their descriptions, go to *drama.eserver.org*.

- Key search words: performing arts center, drama, theatre, community theater, Shakespeare in the Park

Real love—
the lasting kind—
benefits others at the
expense of oneself.

ANONYMOUS

40. Indulge Your Inner Child

Step back to a simpler time and enjoy some of those activities you most liked doing as a child. Go to a park and play on the playground. For dinner, head to the Golden Arches. Order your childhood favorites, and why not treat yourselves to dessert too! After dinner, it's off to the toy store to pick out some of the games and toys you enjoyed when you were little—jacks, hula hoops, a Chinese jump rope, building blocks. Buy a few, and then go home and spend the rest of the evening playing and watching cartoons.

Budget

$-$$ This date shouldn't break the bank, but that all depends on how carried away you get at the toy store!

 Over the Top

- Take a look at some old pictures or videos of each of you as children to add to the evening's nostalgia.

- Visit an antique or collectors' store and see if you can find your favorite toys, just as you remember them.

 Get Connected

Key search words: toys, vintage toys, parks, cartoons

The Coming of Love

It seems to me that the coming of love is like the coming of spring—the date is not to be reckoned by the calendar. It may be slow and gradual; it may be quick and sudden. But in the morning, when we wake and recognize a change in the world without, verdure on the trees, blossoms on the sward, warmth in the sunshine, music in the air, we say spring has come.

EDWARD GEORGE BULWER-LYTTON

41. Take a Float Trip

Fasten your life vest and plunge into a watery adventure. Find a river nearby that is good for floating and rent a canoe, raft, or kayak for the day. If you're new to floating, make sure the river

you choose is beginner friendly and that the establishment you rent your vessel from emphasizes safety. Most rental stores will also offer a ride back to your car when you're finished. Spend the day exploring, enjoying the water, and taking in the fresh air of the great outdoors.

Budget

$$ It's a good idea to check and compare rental rates.

What to Take

- Sunglasses (preferably with straps) and sunscreen

- Insect repellent

- A small first-aid kit

- Plenty of bottled water

- Life vests

- Shoes that fasten tightly on your feet

- Snacks or a picnic lunch

- A waterproof disposable camera

- A watertight container that floats to protect your supplies if your vessel should capsize

 Over the Top

- Take a kayaking or whitewater rafting safety course together, and then head out for a thrilling adventure. Or go on a guided whitewater rafting adventure designed for beginners.

- Purchase your own canoe, kayaks, or raft so you can go floating often.

Get Connected

- Go to *raftingamerica.com* for great information on kayaking and whitewater rafting.

- Go to *nps.gov* or the state park site for your state to find listings of state and national parks in your area that offer canoe, raft, and/or kayak rentals.

- Key search words: canoeing, kayaking, rafting, whitewater rafting

In the eyes of a lover pockmarks are dimples.

JAPANESE PROVERB

42. Create a Furry Friend

Find a store near you where you can build your own stuffed animal, and take your loved one there to create a loveable new friend together. First, pick your animal. There are usually lots to choose from. Then add a sound if you wish. Many of these stores even have a voice box on which you can record your own personal message for the animal to "say."

Next, you'll stuff your animal and name it. See if you can pick a name that has something to do with your relationship. For example, you could name it after the restaurant you went to on your first date, a movie character from a movie you saw together, or a pet name you have for each other. After your new friend has a name, have fun picking out clothes to dress him or her in.

If you enjoy this activity, go back again sometime and make another friend so you'll each have someone to cuddle with when you're apart.

 **Budget**

> $$ If budget is a concern, you may want to agree on a set amount you'll spend beforehand, since it can be easy to get a little carried away. Keep in mind that, if you take your time and enjoy the process, you'll not only get a new furry friend but a full evening of memorable entertainment as well.

Over the Top

Volunteer together to help out at an animal shelter or at the zoo for a day, and gain some new, real furry friends.

 Get Connected

• Visit *buildabear.com* for information about the original build-your-own stuffed animal stores, as well as to find a location near you.

• Key search words: build your own stuffed animal

43. Get Fired Up!

For a fun way to express your creativity, try your hand at painting ceramics. You should be able to find a paint-your-own-pottery studio near you. These studios offer a wide selection of ceramics and pottery pieces for you to choose from. You could paint a decorative item for each of your houses or apartments or something with both form and function, like salt and pepper shakers. Or you could each paint a plate to use anytime you dine in together. After you've chosen your piece, you can use the studio's paints, glazes, and other supplies to complete your masterpieces. Most pieces will then need to be left at the studio to be fired in the kiln. Plan to get together again later in the week to pick up and admire your finished artwork.

Budget

$-$$ Cost will depend upon the pieces you choose. Most studios also charge a small fee for the use of their supplies.

Over the Top

If you're really feeling creative, try taking a pottery class together so you can learn how to do the whole process, from creating a pottery piece from clay to firing it in a kiln, to painting or glazing it.

Get Connected

Key search words: paint your own pottery, pottery studios, pottery classes, ceramics

Put your hand
on a hot stove for a minute
and it seems like an hour,
sit next to a pretty woman for
an hour and it seems like a
minute. That's relativity.

ALBERT EINSTEIN

44. Game Night

For a fun and relaxing night in, don some comfy clothes, pull out some snack foods, and challenge each other at your favorite board or card games.

Who will be the first to arrive at millionaire acres? Which one of you will be the first to put the clues together to find out who did it, with what, and where? Is there a "card shark" in the house? Can you keep your right hand on the red dot, your left foot on the green dot, and your right foot on the yellow dot while reaching over your sweetheart to touch the blue dot with your left hand? Pick several shorter games, or immerse yourself in a longer game you both enjoy.

 **Budget**

$ Unless you decide to buy a new game or stock up on snack foods, this date won't cost a dime!

Over the Top

- Have a trophy made for the winner, or buy some other prize for the champion of the night.

- Go to the store and pick out a new game you've never tried before.

Get Connected

- For game ideas, visit *hasbro.com*, *mattel.com*, or *cranium.com*.

- Key search words: board games, card games

Romance Her

With women,
the little things matter. The
best way to romance her might be
through acts of simple courtesy and
kindness. Open the door for her, help her
out of the car, pull out her chair for her at the
table, properly introduce her to friends and
family, show up on time, turn off your cell
phone when you're with her, keep your
eyes only on her, avoid inappropriate
jokes, respect her values. She'll
call you her prince!

45. Go to a Theme Park

What could be more fun and thrilling than zooming into the air and then plummeting down at breakneck speeds on your favorite roller coaster? Spin, loop, fly, and bounce your way to a great date at a nearby theme park. After you've ridden a few rides, take a break and enjoy some of the in-park entertainment.

Talk about which rides were your favorites when you were a child, and enjoy some snacks while discussing it. While you're there, dare each other to try a ride you've never been on before—one that maybe you've been a little afraid of. If the park offers one, stick around after dark for the light show or fireworks display to top off your exciting day.

 **Budget**

>$$ Since there is a wide range of admission prices for theme parks, check rates before you make plans.

 Over the Top

- Visit one of these top-rated theme parks in the United States: Walt Disney World, Disneyland, Legoland, Busch Gardens, or Universal Studios.

- Try out one of these top-rated European parks: Port Aventura in Barcelona, Chessington or Thorpe Park in London.

Get Connected

- To find theme parks in the United States listed by state, go to *themeparksonline.org*.

- Other good sights for theme park information are *themeparks.about.com* and *themeparkinsider.com*.

- Key search words: theme park followed by your city and state

Keep love in your heart. A life without it is like a sunless garden when the flowers are dead.

OSCAR WILDE

46. Limo Date

Luxurious and romantic—pampering each other with a ride for two in a limo—now that's a date! Although this may be reminiscent of a group of seniors hanging out together on prom night, it's not quite the same when you and your sweetheart go it alone. It's better! Limos are the ultimate in comfort—luxurious leather upholstery, soft romantic lighting, starlite ceiling, color television, and a wonderful sound system to listen to your favorite style of music.

You are dressed in your finest, and you sit back and enjoy being chauffeured as you toast each other with sparkling grape juice. And when you arrive at your dinner destination, you feel like a million dollars as your driver opens your door. Everyone ought to take a spin in a limo just once!

Budget

$$-$$$ Limos are pricey, especially during the holidays and prom seasons. Choosing other times during the year can save you money. Be sure to ask about their package deals. Rental prices will vary according to the length of time you want the limo.

Steps to Success

- Be sure to be on time at the meeting place. You are paying for the time whether you are there or not.

- Check out all the amenities the rental includes.

- Find out whether or not the company owns its own vehicles. If they are the intermediary agent, the price will be higher.

- Ask the company if their vehicles have scheduled maintenance and if they have a contingency plan if your limo has a mechanical problem.

- The rental usually includes beverages. If you want snacks, you may need to take them.

- Ask your driver for suggestions for the best spots for night/holiday lights and sites of interest.

Over the Top

- Instead of going out to dinner, order a gourmet meal from a nice restaurant and eat in the limo while you take in the city's nightly beauty. The rental company may also cater meals.

- Rent a limo for a day tour of a major city.

Get Connected

Key search words: limo rental followed by your town and state, limo day tours, catered gourmet meal followed by your city and state

47. Stargazing

Imagine for a moment that you and your date are entering a planetarium for a very special evening. You take your seats in a dimly lighted room under a great domed ceiling. You lean back in your theater seats and look up as the sky above you darkens. The room is completely black. Then your eyes pick up dots of light, thousands of stars. The calm, relaxed voice of the commentator helps you find Orion and his two dogs, Sirius and Procyon. Above him is Taurus the Bull and the Pleiades. You slip your hand over and take your date's hand. It seems like it's just the two of you, alone under an amazing starscape. What could be more romantic?

Budget

$ Ticket prices tend to be very affordable.

Steps to Success

Recognizing constellations can be challenging at first. But you'll be sure to enjoy the time with your sweetheart under the stars!

Over the Top

- Buy your own telescope and discover the wonder of our galaxy.

- Buy stargazing software and explore on your computer.

Get Connected

Key search words: planetarium followed by
your city and state, telescope, stargazing,
meteor shower, planet gazing

What a grand
thing, to be loved!
What a grander thing still,
to love!

VICTOR HUGO

48. Night Prowl

For a fun nighttime adventure, take a short night hike on a well-traveled trail. Listen carefully and try to identify all of the night sounds—crickets, frogs, locusts, owls, wolves, and coyotes. Make sure to look for lightning bugs along the way. When you get back to your starting point, find a comfortable

place to sit and take turns reading a short story by flashlight. Gaze at the stars and see if you can spot a shooting star.

Budget

$ This is a great date that won't break the bank!

What to Take

- A good flashlight or two and an extra set of batteries

- A whistle and cell phone in case of emergency

- A jacket and comfortable shoes

- An old blanket to sit on and your favorite book of short stories

Steps to Success

- Be sure someone else knows where you'll be, and choose a safe area that's not too isolated.

- Be aware and cautious of wildlife, keeping in mind that many animals are nocturnal and may do their hunting at night.

- Make sure you're allowed to be in the area at night. Many parks have curfews.

Over the Top

Visit one of these top spots for stargazing: Natural Bridges National Monument in Utah, Cape Hatteras National Seashore in North Carolina, Great Basin National Park in Nevada, Bryce Canyon National Park in Utah, Yellowstone National Park in Wyoming, or Crater Lake National Park in Oregon.

Get Connected

Key search words: nocturnal animals, star-gazing, short stories

Four sweet lips,
two pure souls,
and one undying affection—
these are love's pretty
ingredients for a kiss.

CHRISTIAN NESTELL BOVEE

Romance Him

Have you written about
your newest love interest in your
journal? Find an acceptable entry, tear
it out (don't use scissors, you want the
rough-torn look), fold it up and slip it into
his shirt pocket, book bag, somewhere he
is likely to find it. This will be hard on
your journal but soft on his heart.

49. Up, Up, and Away

Very few dates are as impressive as a ride in a hot air balloon, flying high above the landscape, taking in a magnificent view, wind blowing through your hair. Can you imagine it? It is said to be one of the top ten things people want to experience in their lifetimes.

Because of the cost, you may have to save your pennies for a while, but the experience is breathtaking, unforgettable, and perfect for an ultra-special occasion. Some companies offer sweetheart packages, which are flights for two that include items like teddy bears, chocolates, champagne, and fresh flowers. Other packages include breakfast or lunch and lots of great extras. Though tough on the pocketbook, this date is guaranteed to wow just about anyone.

Budget

$$$ Hot air balloon rides can be pricey, so this may be something you'll want to save for an extra special occasion.

What to Take

- Comfortable layered clothing
- Sturdy walking shoes (no high heels, please)
- Camera

Steps to Success

Plan ahead. Almost all balloon rides must be booked no less than a week in advance.

Over the Top

If you decide that he or she is "the one," you can even get married on a hot air balloon! How romantic.

Get Connected

Key search words: hot air balloon ride, sweetheart packages for hot air balloon ride, hot air balloon weddings

50. Treasure Hunt

You may want to make this a group date if you are looking for over-the-top fun and excitement. But it can also be an exceptionally romantic date for two. Present your date with a handwritten clue that leads to another and another and another until the treasure is found. This is a clever way to present Christmas gifts, birthday presents, or gifts of any kind for that matter.

Make your clues romantic and provocative. Using a few lines of well-known love poetry is a good ploy.

Alter a few words here and there to send your date searching in the right direction. Clues can be written on plain index cards or on elaborate creations with frills, bows, and lots of color. Happy hunting!

 Budget

$ Depends completely on the cost of the treasure. Add a few dollars for materials for creating beautiful clue cards. Also include gas money if your hunt extends any distance from your starting place.

 Over the Top

• For the latest in treasure hunts, try geocaching. This is a game people play using GPS (global positioning system) devices in order to find caches left by others in different areas.

- A cache usually consists of a logbook which will have valuable information such as facts about the area, perhaps some jokes, and maybe even clues to the whereabouts of the next cache. It may also contain small items of interest.

- A GPS device will cost between $100 and $1000.

 Get Connected

- Check out *geocaching.com* for everything you need to know about geocaching.

- Key search words: treasure hunt, scavenger hunt, geocaching, GPS device

51. Play in the Rain

Remember when you were a kid and playing in the rain was a fun thing to do? Stomping through a puddle in our best shoes or sticking our tongues out to catch the raindrops just seemed like a great idea.

"We had a lot more fun back then," you might say—and you'd be right.

So how about a great impromptu date where the two of you forget about acting like proper adults and embrace the childish and immature approach to a rain shower. Throw off the rain slickers and umbrellas, kick off your shoes, and soak in the rain like the trees and shrubs and flowers do—with gusto. Twirl, dance, dash, splash! When you're all through, dry off, change clothes, and share a PB&J sandwich and pudding cups. It's good to be kids again, and it's even better to do it together!

Budget

$ Rain? God doesn't charge a dime for rain!

What to Take

- Rain-worthy shoes and clothing

- Beach towel

- Clothes to change into later

- Lunch items you loved as a kid

- Juice boxes to go with lunch

Get Connected

Key search words: weather forecast followed by your city and state

52. Fly a Kite

Sun, fun, and the great outdoors. Those are just
a few of the reasons to stand next to your date,
bobbin of string in hand, and watch your kite float
high above your heads. As it dips, weaves, and
soars, you'll feel as if the two of you are doing
the same. It's mesmerizing. Take turns holding the
bobbin and feel free to experiment, seeing if you
can make your kite go this way or that. Reel it
in and let it back out. Run in the opposite direction and watch it follow—an absolute exercise in
whimsy.

Take a picnic lunch with you to the park and wile
the day away making pretty circles in the sky. It's
fun for one—and even more fun for two!

Budget

$-$$ You can spend quite a lot for a kite or
next to nothing. The more expensive ones
are often sturdier and more likely to be used
again. But the simple, inexpensive variety
will give you hours of fun for just a few
dollars.

What to Take

- A kite

- Comfortable clothes and running shoes

- Sunscreen, sunglasses, and a hat

- Blanket and picnic basket

- Camera

Steps to Success

Remember these rules for flying a kite safely:

- Stay away from power lines.

- Don't try to fly kites in a storm or rainy weather (just ask Ben Franklin)!

- Choose an open field, meadow, or park where you can steer clear of trees.

- Use the string that comes with your kite or an approved type of kite line.

Over the Top

Enter a kite-flying competition.

Get Connected

Key search words: kite, kite flying, kite-flying competition

Also look for this book:

HOWARD BOOKS
A DIVISION OF SIMON & SCHUSTER
New York   London   Toronto   Sydney